JOB

Clifford M. Yeary

A ministry of the Diocese of Little Rock
in partnership with Liturgical Press

DIOCESE OF LITTLE ROCK

2500 North Tyler Street • P.O. Box 7565 • Little Rock, Arkansas 72217 • (501) 664-0340 Fax (501) 664-6304

Dear Friends in Christ,

Sacred Scripture is a wealth of inspired wisdom express-ing Christian truths which challenge us to deepen our relationship with God. Although the Bible can be intimi-dating, it is important that we study God's word in the Scriptures, because it is the basis of our faith and offers us the thoughts and experiences of Christians past and present. It is God speaking to us through the insights of Church fathers and later saints.

I am pleased to present this study guide from Little Rock Scripture Study to serve as an aid for reflection and con-templation in your reading of Scripture. At the same time, the guide will give you insight into how to apply what you have read to your life today.

I encourage you to read Sacred Scripture slowly and reflectively so that it can penetrate your heart and mind. It is my hope that the Word of God will empower you as Christians to live a life worthy of your call as a child of God and a member of the body of Christ.

Sincerely in Christ,

✝ Anthony B. Taylor
Bishop of Little Rock

Sacred Scripture

"The Church has always venerated the divine Scriptures just as she venerates the body of the Lord, since from the table of both the word of God and of the body of Christ she unceasingly receives and offers to the faithful the bread of life, especially in the sacred liturgy. She has always regarded the Scriptures together with sacred tradition as the supreme rule of faith, and will ever do so. For, inspired by God and committed once and for all to writing, they impart the word of God Himself without change, and make the voice of the Holy Spirit resound in the words of the prophets and apostles. Therefore, like the Christian religion itself, all the preaching of the Church must be nourished and ruled by sacred Scripture. For in the sacred books, the Father who is in heaven meets His children with great love and speaks with them; and the force and power in the word of God is so great that it remains the support and energy of the Church, the strength of faith for her sons, the food of the soul, the pure and perennial source of spiritual life."

Vatican II, Dogmatic Constitution on Divine Revelation, no. 21.

INTERPRETATION OF SACRED SCRIPTURE

"Since God speaks in sacred Scripture through men in human fashion, the interpreter of sacred Scripture, in order to see clearly what God wanted to communicate to us, should carefully investigate what meaning the sacred writers really intended, and what God wanted to manifest by means of their words.

"Those who search out the intention of the sacred writers must, among other things, have regard for 'literary forms.' For truth is proposed and expressed in a variety of ways, depending on whether a text is history of one kind or another, or whether its form is that of prophecy, poetry, or some other type of speech. The interpreter must investigate what meaning the sacred writer intended to express and actually expressed in particular circumstances as he used contemporary literary forms in accordance with the situation of his own time and culture.

For the correct understanding of what the sacred author wanted to assert, due attention must be paid to the customary and characteristic styles of perceiving, speaking, and narrating which prevailed at the time of the sacred writer, and to the customs men normally followed in that period in their everyday dealings with one another."

Vatican II, Dogmatic Constitution on Divine Revelation, no. 12.

Instructions

MATERIALS FOR THE STUDY

This Study Guide: Job

Commentary: The New Collegeville Bible Commentary, Old Testament, Volume 19, *Job*, by Kathleen M. O'Connor (Liturgical Press), is used with this study. The abbreviation for this commentary, NCBC-OT VOLUME 19, and the assigned pages are found at the beginning of each lesson.

Bible: We highly recommend the *Little Rock Catholic Study Bible* (Liturgical Press), although any version of the New American Bible, Revised Edition (NABRE), or the New Jerusalem Bible will suffice. Paraphrased editions are discouraged as they offer little, if any, help when facing difficult textual questions. Choose a Bible you feel free to write in or underline.

WEEKLY LESSONS

Lesson 1—Job 1–3
Lesson 2—Job 4–10
Lesson 3—Job 11–19
Lesson 4—Job 20–28
Lesson 5—Job 29–37
Lesson 6—Job 38–42

YOUR DAILY PERSONAL STUDY

The first step is prayer. Open your heart and mind to God. Reading Scripture is an opportunity to listen to God who loves you. Pray that the same Holy Spirit who guided the formation of Scripture will inspire you to correctly understand what you read and empower you to make what you read a part of your life.

The next step is commitment. Daily spiritual food is as necessary as food for the body. This study is divided into daily units. Schedule a regular time and place for your study, as free from distractions as possible. Allow about twenty minutes a day. Make it a daily appointment with God.

As you begin each lesson read the indicated pages of the commentary and the appropriate Scripture passages where indicated. This preparation will give you an overview of the entire lesson and help you to appreciate the context of individual passages.

As you reflect on Scripture, ask yourself these four questions:

1. *What does the Scripture passage say?*
   Read the passage slowly and reflectively. Use your imagination to picture the scene or enter into it.

2. *What does the Scripture passage mean?*
   Read the footnotes and the commentary to help you understand what the sacred writers intended and what God wanted to communicate by means of their words.

3. *What does the Scripture passage mean to me?*
   Meditate on the passage. God's Word is living and powerful. What is God saying to you today? How does the Scripture passage apply to your life today?

4. *What am I going to do about it?*
   Try to discover how God may be challenging you in this passage. An encounter with God contains a challenge to know God's will and follow it more closely in daily life.

THE QUESTIONS ASSIGNED FOR EACH DAY

Read the questions and references for each day. The questions are designed to help you listen to God's Word and to prepare you for the weekly small-group discussion.

Some of the questions can be answered briefly and objectively by referring to the Bible references and the commentary *(What does the passage say?)*. Some will lead you to a better understanding of how the Scriptures apply to the Church, sacraments, and society *(What does the passage mean?)*. Some questions will invite you to consider how God's Word challenges or supports you in your relationships with God and others *(What does the passage mean to me?)*. Finally, the questions will lead you to examine your actions in light of Scripture *(What am I going to do about it?)*.

Write your responses in this study guide or in a notebook to help you clarify and organize your thoughts and feelings.

THE WEEKLY SMALL-GROUP MEETING

The weekly small-group sharing is the heart of the Little Rock Scripture Study Program. Participants gather in small groups to share the results of praying, reading, and reflecting on Scripture and on the assigned questions. The goal of the discussion is for group members to be strengthened and nourished individually and as a community through sharing how God's Word speaks to them and affects their daily lives. The daily study questions will guide the discussion; it is not necessary to discuss all the questions.

All members share the responsibility of creating an atmosphere of loving support and trust in the group by respecting the opinions and experiences of others, and by affirming and encouraging one another. The simple shared prayer that begins and ends each small group meeting also helps create the open and trusting environment in which group members can share their faith deeply and grow in the study of God's Word.

A distinctive feature of this program is its emphasis on and trust in God's presence working in and through each member. Sharing responses to God's presence in the Word and in others can bring about remarkable growth and transformation.

THE WRAP-UP LECTURE

The lecture is designed to develop and clarify the themes of each lesson. It is not intended to be the focus of the group's discussion. For this reason, the lecture always occurs *after* the small group discussion. If several small groups meet at one time, the groups may gather in a central location to listen to the lecture.

Lectures may be presented by a local speaker. They are also available in audio form on CD, and in visual form on DVD.

Job 1–3

NCBC-OT VOLUME 19, PAGES 5–17

Day 1

1. What do you hope to gain (or learn) from studying the book of Job?

2. According to the commentary's introduction, the story of Job gives vivid testimony to what?

3. What makes Job a classic of world literature?

Day 2

4. Much of Job is a lamentation. What are the literary characteristics of a lament?

5. Why is Job considered to be one of the Bible's books of Wisdom literature?

6. How does the book of Job reflect the importance of honor and shame in Israel's culture?

Day 3

7. How is Job's character described in 1:1?

8. What is the importance of Job's wealth in relation to his moral character (1:2-3)? (See Gen 13:2; Deut 30:15-16.)

9. How did Job show his concern for his children's spiritual welfare (1:4-5)?

Day 4

10. Who are the sons of God who present themselves before the Lord (1:6)? (See Ps 109:6; Zech 3:1.)

11. Who is "the satan" that appears before God (1:6-12)?

12. Why does God allow the satan to bring disaster to Job's livestock, his servants, and his children (1:9-12)?

Day 5

13. What is Job's response to the news of the catastrophes that have destroyed his possessions and killed his children (1:13-21)?

14. What is the satan's purpose in proposing "skin for skin" (2:1-6)?

15. Why would Job's wife respond to his personal suffering as she does (2:7-10)?

Day 6

16. a) Why do Job's friends come to him (2:11)?

    b) How do Job's friends respond to the sight of Job (2:12-13)?

17. In some cultures people demonstrate their grief with physical gestures of lament (2:12). (See 1:20; 2:8; 1 Sam 4:12; Jdt 8:4-6; Esth C:12-13.) Discuss whether or not you see a value in public lament. Why?

18. As Job curses the day he was born, which verses do you find the most moving, or perhaps painful, to reflect upon (3:1-26)?

Job 4–10

NCBC-OT VOLUME 19, PAGES 18–33

Day 1

1. From last week's lesson (Job 1–3), what character other than Job most stirred your interest?

2. How does Eliphaz describe Job's character before Job's many tragedies (4:1-6)?

3. What does Eliphaz seek to remind Job concerning God's dealings with humans (4:7-11)?

Day 2

4. How does Eliphaz describe the circumstances in which he believes he was spoken to by God (4:12-16)? (See 1 Kgs 19:9-12.)

5. In what ways have you ever sensed that God was speaking to you?

6. What was the message that Eliphaz heard (4:17-21)?

Day 3

7. a) How does Eliphaz describe the involvement of God in human affairs in 5:8-13? (See 1 Sam 2:7-8; Ps 113:7; Luke 1:52; 1 Cor 3:19.)

    b) Is there any danger in Eliphaz's assumptions?

8. What does Job tell his friends that he wants from God (6:8-10)?

9. Why does Job accuse his friends of being undependable (6:14-25)?

Day 4

10. Compare Job's prayer in 7:11-21 with Psalm 8. What makes these two prayers so different and yet ironically alike?

11. a) How does Bildad explain the death of Job's children (8:4)?

    b) As opposed to Bildad's lack of sensitivity, give an example, if you can, of someone who gave real comfort to another in a time of loss.

12. Bildad encourages Job to rely on the tried-and-true wisdom of his ancestors (8:8-10). What examples can you give of folk wisdom that might not be as wise or foolproof as modern approaches? (See Matt 9:17.)

Day 5

13. a) What does Bildad imply about Job when he tells him about the fate of the wicked (8:11-19)?

    b) In what way does Bildad offer encouragement to Job (8:21-22)?

14. Job feels threatened by God's greatness (9:4-11), whereas the psalmist (Ps 104) rejoices in God's majesty. What, in your faith, causes you to sense the most joy in God's presence?

15. What does Job's suffering lead him to conclude about God's justice in the world (9:22-24)? (See Eccl 7:15; 8:14; Matt 5:44-45.)

Day 6

16. Why might Christians see Jesus as an answer to Job's lament in 9:33-35? (See 1 Tim 2:5-6; 1 John 2:1-2.)

17. When have you ever prayed with boldness to God, perhaps, like Job, even demanding a response (10:1-7)? (See Luke 11:5-10.)

18. Job's prayer in 10:8-13 reflects a change from his lament in 3:1-13. What do you believe are some reasons his prayer would change?

Job 11–19

NCBC-OT VOLUME 19, PAGES 33–49

Day 1

1. Based on last week's lesson, what have Job's friends been telling him is the cause of his suffering?

2. What course of action (11:13-17) does Zophar tell Job will lead him back to a life "brighter than the noonday"?

3. When have you experienced being wrongly judged in a negative manner? How did you respond?

Day 2

4. Job's suffering has also led to his being disrespected by his peers (12:4-5). Where do you see those who suffer today also being disrespected as a result?

5. How is the disrespect shown Job (12:4-5) similar to the experience of Christ in his suffering (Matt 27:42; Mark 10:33-34)?

6. What signs can you find in Job's speech in 13:1-21 that he still has a deep reverence for God?

Day 3

7. Based on Job's laments in 14:1-14, what is his understanding of the afterlife? (See 3:11-19; Ps 88:11-13; 115:17.)

8. How do Job's misgivings about human destiny in 14:12 compare with what is proclaimed in Daniel 12:2-3?

9. In deriding Job's lack of wisdom, Eliphaz asks him if he considers himself "the first to be born" (15:7). In Old Testament Wisdom literature, who is the firstborn of creation? (See Prov 8:12-25; Wis 9:9.)

Day 4

10. a) What is the teaching that Eliphaz claims the wise have related without contradiction "since the days of their ancestors" (15:18-35)?

   b) What does your life experience teach you about this matter?

11. While he utterly rejects what his friends are telling him, what does Job say that suggests he once thought like his friends about God's justice (16:1-5)?

12. How does Job let his friends know that he has not thoroughly given up hope of being found innocent before God (16:18-21)?

Day 5

13. a) Who do you think is Job's advocate (16:19)?

   b) When have you been an advocate for someone in need (or perhaps someone was an advocate for you in a time of need)?

14. What lies at the very heart of Job's lament (16:21)?

15. Job experiences anguish at being reviled by the good people of his society (17:1-7). What do you think are the greatest sufferings of those who have been falsely accused or incriminated in our society, and what might we owe them?

Day 6

16. Bildad describes in great detail the punishment in this life that he believes falls on "the one who does not know God!" (18:1-21). On the positive side, what are the rewards you have been given as a result of the gift of faith?

17. What great hope does Job express in 19:25-27? (See the NABRE footnote to these verses.)

18. Against whom is Job warning of vengeance (19:28-29)?

Job 20–28

NCBC-OT VOLUME 19, PAGES 49–65

Day 1

1. As you think over the discussion or questions from last week's lesson, what stands out most in your mind?

2. What does ancient wisdom teach that Zophar claims Job has never learned (20:4-5)? (See Ps 37:10.)

3. According to Zophar, what is the chief crime of the wicked for which they are punished (20:19)? (See Deut 15:11; Prov 14:31.)

Day 2

4. How do you deal with apparent inequalities (injustices) when you notice them (21:7-13)? (See Eccl 8:14.)

5. Why do you think Job expresses such concern for the lack of punishment meted out to the wicked in their lifetimes (21:7-34)?

6. a) What crimes does Eliphaz accuse Job of committing (22:1-11)?

   b) How does he suggest Job might become free of his punishment (22:21-30)?

Day 3

7. a) Job says that "today" his complaint is especially bitter (23:1-5). What does he seem to desire most from God at this point?

   b) When in your spiritual life have you found it especially difficult to find God's presence (23:3)?

8. How confident is Job of his case with God (23:4-10)?

9. What is at the heart of Job's complaint in 24:1?

Day 4

10. a) What are the evils in human society that Job bewails (24:1-15)?

    b) To what extent does his list still summarize the evils of the world?

11. How would you sum up Bildad's latest response (25:1-6) to Job's assertions concerning God and justice (24:1-25)?

12. Bildad asks, "How can anyone be in the right against God, or how can any born of woman be innocent?" (Job 25:4). What good news does Paul find in the universality of human sinfulness (Rom 3:21-26)?

Day 5

13. Job gives a very sarcastic reply to Bildad, who has accused Job of sin (25:1–26:4). In your experience, what causes many arguments to break down into disrespect?

14. Who or what is this "Rahab" that God has crushed (26:12)? (See Job 9:13; Ps 89:11; Isa 59:11; and NABRE footnote to Job 26:12.)

15. What are some of the marvels of creation (26:8-13) that give you pause when thinking of them as "but the outlines of his ways," or just "a whisper of a word we hear of him" (26:14)?

Day 6

16. Why is the section found in 27:7-23 said to be inconsistent with Job's previous arguments (as in 27:1-6)?

17. Who or what have been the greatest sources of wisdom for you (28:1-28, esp. v. 12)?

18. What are the great values of your life, for which "[s]olid gold cannot purchase" (28:15-19)?

Job 29–37

NCBC-OT VOLUME 19, PAGES 66–83

Day 1

1. What do you recall from last week's lesson that best illustrates for you the depth of Job's predicament?

2. Job becomes nostalgic as he remembers the joys of his former life (29:1-13). What would you consider to be your "good old days" (and why)?

3. In what ways does your faith community perform the righteous deeds of being "eyes to the blind" or "feet to the lame," or otherwise serve the poor and the stranger (29:15-16)?

Day 2

4. a) Who in our communities are often made victims of the kind of abuse and bullying to which Job has become prey (30:9-14)?

   b) What are some practical ways to prevent bullying?

5. What signs do scholars find in Job's speech (31:1-40) that he is preparing a legal case before God?

6. Job's oaths of innocence are also signs of an examination of conscience. What role in your own spiritual life has examining your conscience played?

Day 3

7. a) Why do many scholars regard Elihu's speeches (32:1–37:24) to be a later insertion into the book of Job?

   b) What purpose might Elihu's speeches serve as part of Job's story?

8. What has driven Elihu to confront Job and the three friends (32:6b-16)?

9. According to Elihu, how have Job's responses to his predicament given offense to God (33:8-12)?

Day 4

10. Elihu sees suffering as God's attempt to turn people away from sin. What message does this send about Elihu's understanding of God (33:17-30)? (See 2 Pet 3:9.)

11. What are the blasphemies Elihu accuses Job of committing (34:7-12)? (See 9:22-23, 30-31.)

12. What has Job done to cause Elihu to accuse him of rebellion (34:37)?

Day 5

13. In chapter 35, does Elihu describe a God who is transcendent and detached or a God who is reachable and involved?

14. If, as Elihu says, our sins or good deeds can't take anything away from or add to God (35:6-7), why are they important to God?

15. a) Elihu believes he is speaking for or defending God (36:2). When have you ever felt it necessary to defend God or hoped that someone would?

    b) Have you ever felt that a "defense" of God or religion went over the line?

Day 6

16. a) How does Job's experience argue against Elihu's eloquent theological claims (36:5-15)?

    b) When have you ever had to trust your own experience over someone else's well-reasoned logic?

17. Elihu senses God's marvels in thunder and lightning (36:32–37:5). What marvels of the world or universe stir awe in your heart for God's power? (See Ps 29.)

18. The "fear of God" is very important in Scripture (37:23-24). (See Deut 6:24; Prov 1:7; Sir 25:11.)

    a) What is meant by the fear of the Lord?

    b) What is more important than fearing God? (See John 15:14-15; 1 John 4:18.)

Job 38–42

NCBC-OT VOLUME 19, PAGES 83–105

Day 1

1. Looking back at last week's lesson, if Elihu had asked for your advice, what would you have counseled him to say to Job?

2. Considering Job's previous lament at being ignored by God (23:2-9), how do you imagine Job would have first reacted at suddenly being answered by God "out of the storm" (38:1)?

3. How might the imagery God uses of birthing the world (38:8-9, 29) be part of an answer to Job's complaints concerning God's aloofness (23:2-9)? (See Gen 1:9-10; Ps 33:6-9.)

Day 2

4. As you ponder creation, what aspects of God's providential care most stir your thoughts (38:22-41)? (See Ps 19:2-6; 104:24-30; Rom 1:19-20.)

5. God probes Job about his knowledge of the beasts (Job 39:1-30). What is your favorite creature of the wild? How did it come to be your favorite?

6. It is said that in just a few decades, the vast majority of all people on earth will live in cities. What can city planners do to ensure that people are aware of the wonders of nature as described in Job 39:1-30?

Day 3

7. In what ways have you recently experienced God responding to your prayers (40:1)?

8. Why would Job finally go silent now that he has an audience with God (40:3-5)?

9. Are you satisfied with Job's response to God (40:3-5)? If you experienced what Job had, how might you have responded, or what questions would you have asked God?

Day 4

10. What in God's challenge to Job suggests that God has, after all, been listening to Job's laments (40:8)?

11. a) What are the creatures called Behemoth (40:15-24) and Leviathan (40:25–41:26)? (See 3:8; 7:12; Ps 74:14; 104:26; Isa 27:1.)

    b) Why are these creatures so important to God's interrogation of Job?

12. In what way is God's description of the mighty Behemoth and Leviathan (40:15–41:26) said to change "everything" for Job (commentary, p. 96)?

Day 5

13. a) How important has it been to Job to actually "see" (have a direct encounter with) God (42:5)? (See 19:25-27; 23:2-3.)

    b) How important to your own spirituality is the desire to dwell in God's presence?

14. What religious experiences (including those springing from your sacramental life) have helped affirm you in your faith in difficult times?

15. What has Job done for which he must repent (42:5-6)?

Day 6

16. a) How satisfying to you is Job's restoration to health and wealth as a conclusion to his story?

    b) What lingering questions do you have about Job's suffering or God's response?

17. In what ways has studying Job affected how you think about God's care for all creatures and the problem of suffering in the world?

18. In what ways might a careful, faithful reading of Job affect how local faith communities respond to suffering in their midst?

ABBREVIATIONS

Books of the Bible

Gen—Genesis
Exod—Exodus
Lev—Leviticus
Num—Numbers
Deut—Deuteronomy
Josh—Joshua
Judg—Judges
Ruth—Ruth
1 Sam—1 Samuel
2 Sam—2 Samuel
1 Kgs—1 Kings
2 Kgs—2 Kings
1 Chr—1 Chronicles
2 Chr—2 Chronicles
Ezra—Ezra
Neh—Nehemiah
Tob—Tobit
Jdt—Judith
Esth—Esther
1 Macc—1 Maccabees
2 Macc—2 Maccabees
Job—Job
Ps(s)—Psalm(s)
Prov—Proverbs
Eccl—Ecclesiastes
Song—Song of Songs
Wis—Wisdom
Sir—Sirach
Isa—Isaiah
Jer—Jeremiah
Lam—Lamentations
Bar—Baruch
Ezek—Ezekiel
Dan—Daniel
Hos—Hosea
Joel—Joel
Amos—Amos

Obad—Obadiah
Jonah—Jonah
Mic—Micah
Nah—Nahum
Hab—Habakkuk
Zeph—Zephaniah
Hag—Haggai
Zech—Zechariah
Mal—Malachi
Matt—Matthew
Mark—Mark
Luke—Luke
John—John
Acts—Acts
Rom—Romans
1 Cor—1 Corinthians
2 Cor—2 Corinthians
Gal—Galatians
Eph—Ephesians
Phil—Philippians
Col—Colossians
1 Thess—1 Thessalonians
2 Thess—2 Thessalonians
1 Tim—1 Timothy
2 Tim—2 Timothy
Titus—Titus
Phlm—Philemon
Heb—Hebrews
Jas—James
1 Pet—1 Peter
2 Pet—2 Peter
1 John—1 John
2 John—2 John
3 John—3 John
Jude—Jude
Rev—Revelation